W9-CZK-592

The Night Sky

Kimberly M. Hutmacher

Science Content Editor:
Shirley Duke

Educational Media

rourkeeducationalmedia.com

Scan for Related Titles
and Teacher Resources

Science Content Editor: Shirley Duke holds a bachelor's degree in biology and a master's degree in education from Austin College in Sherman, Texas. She taught science in Texas at all levels for twenty-five years before starting to write for children. Her science books include *You Can't Wear These Genes, Infections, Infestations, and Diseases, Enterprise STEM, Forces and Motion at Work, Environmental Disasters,* and *Gases.* She continues writing science books and also works as a science content editor.

www.rourkeeducationalmedia.com

Photo credits: Cover © Orla, Igor Kovalchuk, Snaprender; Pages 2/3 © jupeart; Pages 4/5 © sebikus; Pages 6/7 © Andrew F. Kazmierski, pjmorley; Pages 8/9 © godrick, Viktar Malyshchyts, Bob Orsillo; Pages 10/11 © Primož Cigler, oorka; Pages 12/13 © NASA, Giovanni Benintende; Pages 14/15 © courtesy of ESO astronomer Yuri Beletsky, jupeart, olly; Pages 16/17 © NASA, silver tiger; Pages 18/19 © shooarts, ella1977; Pages 20/21 © Kostyantyn Ivanyshen, Mark R

Editor: Kelli Hicks

My Science Library series produced by Blue Door Publishing, Florida for Rourke Educational Media.

Library of Congress PCN Data

Hutmacher, Kimberly M.
 The Night Sky / Kimberly M. Hutmacher.
   p. cm. -- (My Science Library)
 ISBN 978-1-61810-092-4 (Hard cover) (alk. paper)
 ISBN 978-1-61810-225-6 (Soft cover)
 Library of Congress Control Number: 2011943575

Rourke Educational Media
Printed in the United States of America,
North Mankato, Minnesota

Also Available as:

rourkeeducationalmedia.com

customerservice@rourkeeducationalmedia.com
PO Box 643328 Vero Beach, Florida 32964

Table of Contents

Hello Neighbor!

Earth's closest neighbor in space is the Moon. Earth orbits the Sun, and the Moon orbits Earth. Did you know that the Moon doesn't give off its own light? The Moon's glow comes from sunlight reflecting off its surface.

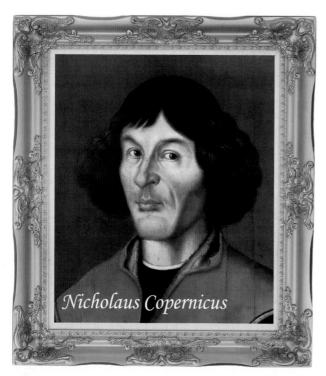

Nicholaus Copernicus

It was once thought that Earth was at the center of our solar system. In 1543, Nicholaus Copernicus published his revolutionary theory that placed the Sun at the center of our solar system.

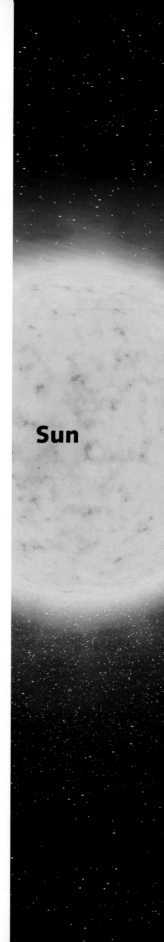

Sun

Astronomers are scientists who study the universe. They think the Moon used to be part of Earth. Billions of years ago, a large body from space crashed into Earth, breaking off large chunks. Scientists believe the large chunks later joined together and hardened to form our Moon.

Moon

Earth

Shapes of the Moon

When we look at the Moon throughout the month, it appears to change shape. It doesn't change shape, though. It only looks that way to us because we see different parts of it lit by the Sun. The same side of the Moon always faces Earth. As it orbits we see different shapes called **moon phases**.

The Moon and Tides

The waves wash up regularly both at high tide and low tide. The level to which they extend moves higher up the shore during high tide and recedes more at low tide because of the Moon's pull.

Each week of the month, the Moon circles about one-fourth of the way around Earth. When Earth passes between the Sun and Moon, and the Moon's lit side is facing Earth, we see a full Moon.

A week later, the Moon has turned so that we only see half its reflecting light.

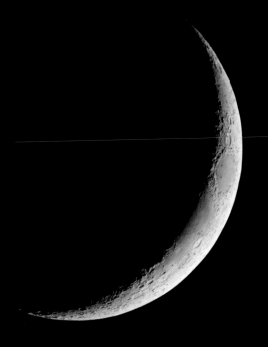

Another week later, only a sliver of the Moon in a crescent shape is lit.

The fourth week, we see a new Moon. The Moon passes between the Sun and Earth, and the Sun shines on the side of the Moon facing away from Earth. It looks like the Moon has disappeared! The Moon is still there, though. We just can't see it.

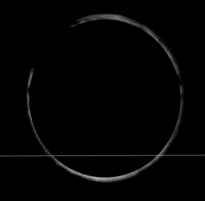

Earth only has one Moon, but more than one hundred and forty moons have been discovered around other planets in our **solar system**.

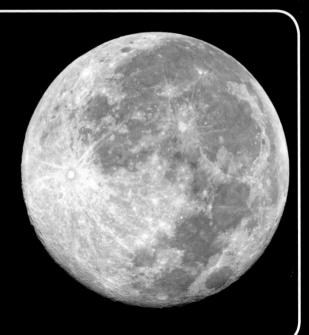

Casting Shadows

During a **lunar eclipse**, the Moon passes behind Earth, blocking the Sun's rays. Sometimes this casts a shadow on the Moon.

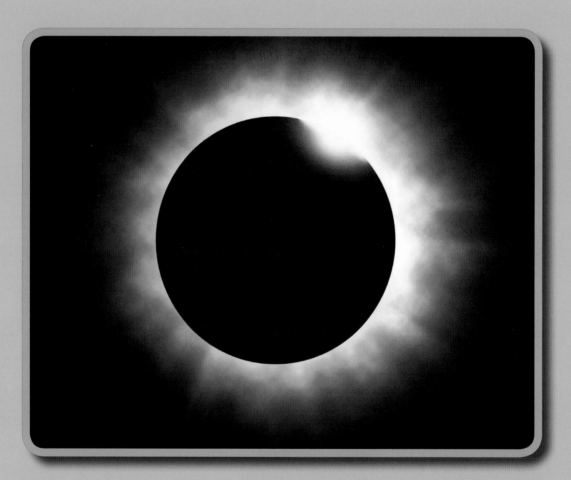

A solar eclipse happens when the Moon is between the Sun and Earth, and the Moon's shadow falls on Earth.

This photo shows a lunar eclipse from 2007. A lunar eclipse takes place two to four times a year.

Dust, Rocks, and Snow

Asteroids are space rocks that orbit the Sun. Billions of asteroids make up the Main Belt. It takes three to six years for each asteroid to orbit the Sun.

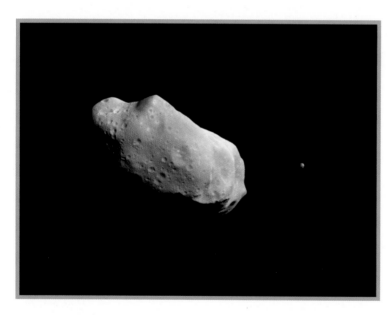

Most of the asteroids in our solar system are located in the Main Belt between the orbits of Mars and Jupiter.

comet

A **comet** is a small space object made of snow, ice, and dust. It's nicknamed *the dirty snowball*. A **meteoroid** is a chunk, or a small piece of dust, from a comet or asteroid. The light made by a meteoroid passing through Earth's atmosphere is called a **meteor**.

A Star is Born

Billions of stars also light our night sky. Stars are huge balls of hot, glowing gas that shine throughout our universe. The Sun is not the brightest star, but it seems like it to us because it's the closest one to Earth.

All of the stars in our **galaxy** belong to a group called the Milky Way. It's called the Milky Way because, grouped together, the stars look like a long stream of milk.

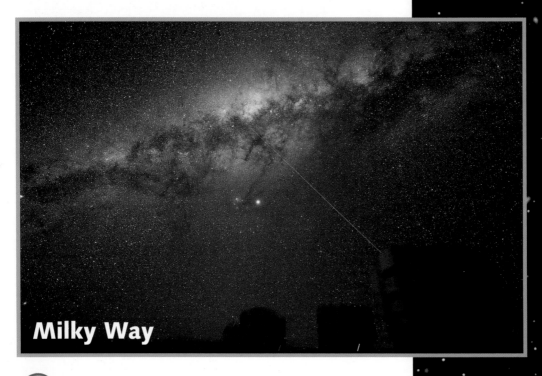

Milky Way

Stars come in many sizes. Some are 100 to 200 times larger than the Sun, while others are smaller than Earth.

Scientists use a telescope to view the night sky.

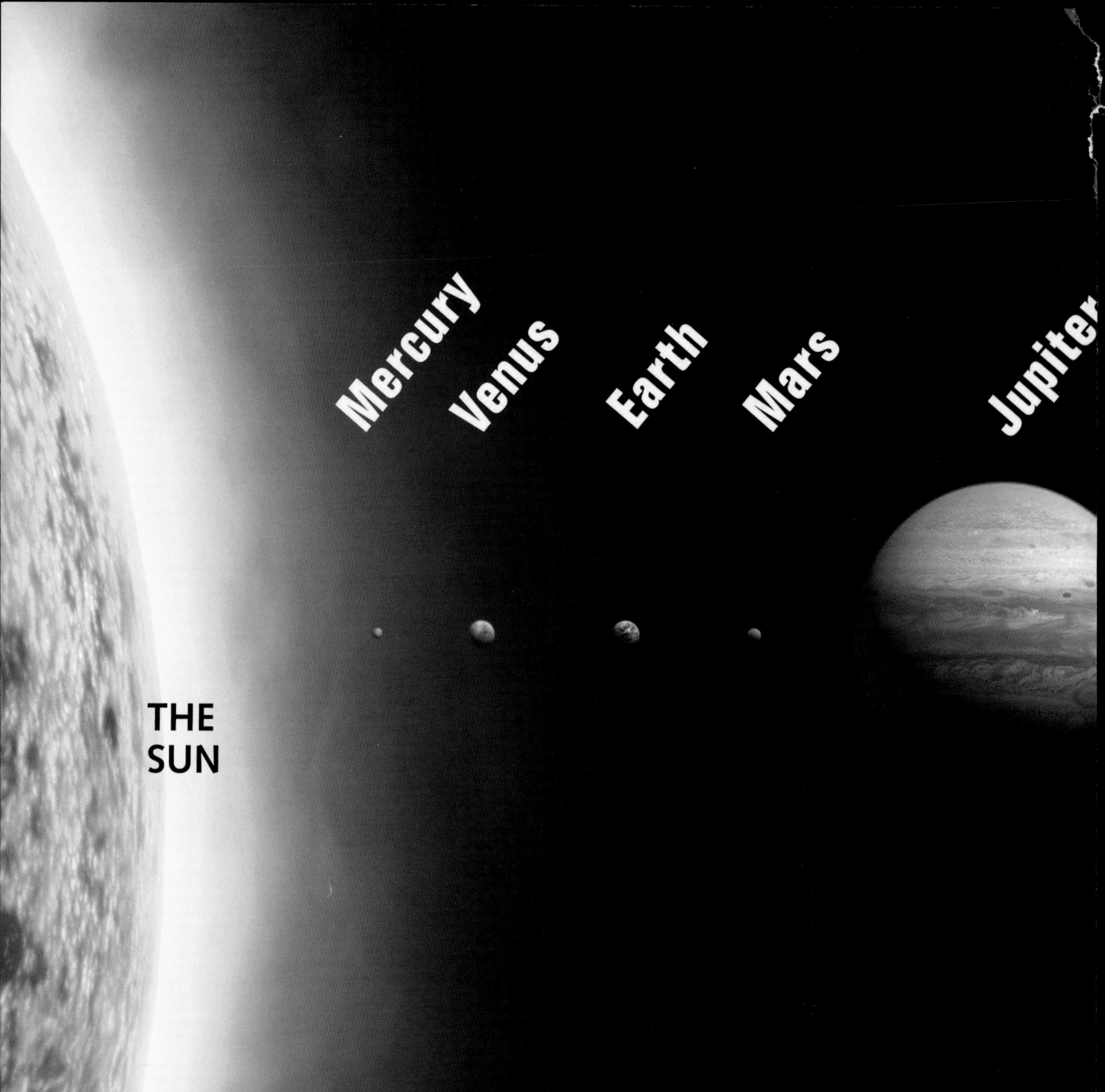

Mercury

Venus

Earth

Mars

Jupiter

**THE
SUN**

Planets orbit stars and get their light
from that star as they rotate and revolve
around it. Earth orbits the Sun, a medium-
sized star. Earth rotates toward the east,
so that the Sun rises in the east and sets in
the west.

Our solar system is made up of all of the planets that orbit the Sun, along with moons, comets, asteroids, smaller minor planets, dust, and gas.

Saturn

Uranus

Neptune

It takes one full year for Earth to orbit the Sun.

Pictures in the Sky

Long ago, people noticed that certain stars, grouped together, formed pictures of people, animals, and objects in the sky. These pictures are called **constellations**, and the ancient Romans gave the constellations names.

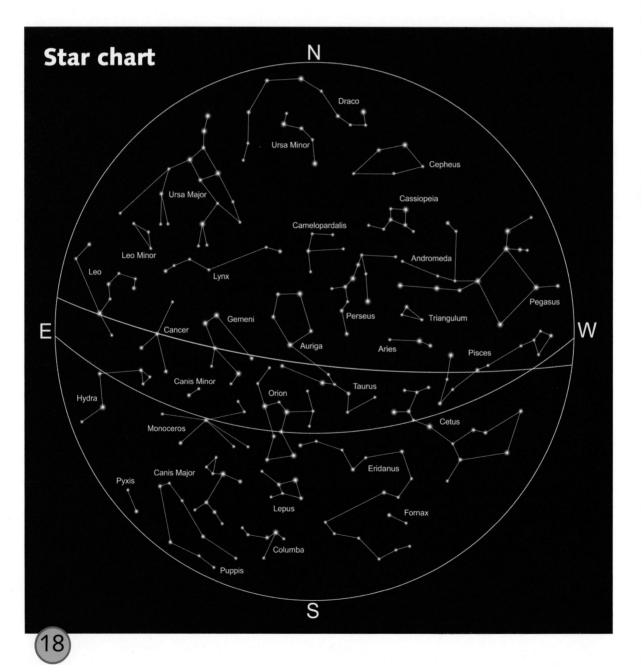

Star chart

N

Draco

Ursa Minor

Cepheus

Ursa Major

Cassiopeia

Camelopardalis

Andromeda

Leo Minor

Pegasus

Leo

Lynx

Perseus

Triangulum

Gemeni

E

Cancer

Aries

Pisces

W

Auriga

Canis Minor

Taurus

Hydra

Orion

Cetus

Monoceros

Canis Major

Eridanus

Pyxis

Lepus

Fornax

Columba

Puppis

S

Astronomers make star charts. Star charts are maps of the night sky, and we can use them to find constellations.

The Big Dipper is in the constellation of Ursa Major. The Little Dipper, also called Ursa Minor, looks like a soup ladle. The star at the end of its handle is Polaris, also called the North Star.

North Star (Polaris)

The Little Dipper (Ursa Minor)

Orion looks like a hunter with a club, shield, and belt. Near Orion, we see Canis Major, also known as the Greater Dog.

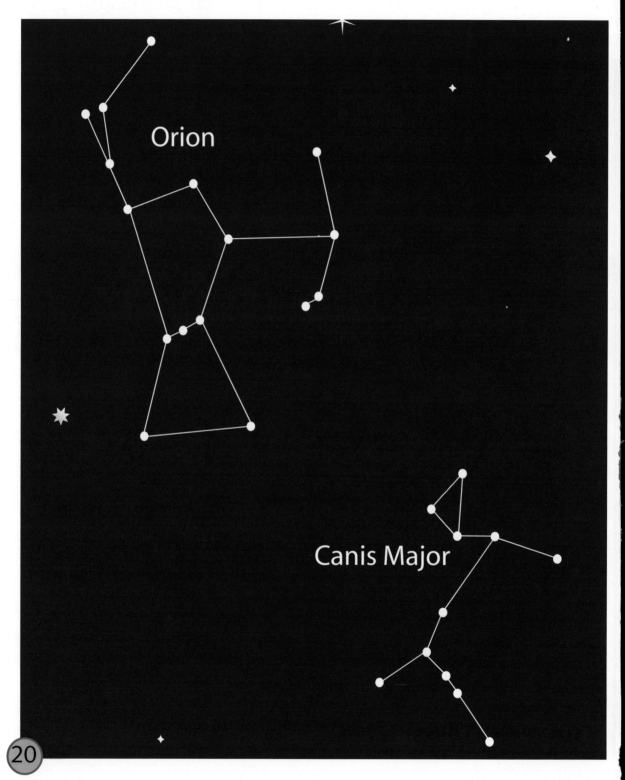

Orion

Canis Major

For thousands of years, stars have helped us **navigate** where we want to go and helped us keep track of time. The night sky is not only beautiful, but useful too!

Show What You Know

1. Does the Moon really give off its own light? If not, where does the light on the Moon come from?

2. What are the names of two constellations described in this book?

3. What does an astronomer do?

Glossary

asteroids (AS-tuh-roidz): space rocks that orbit the Sun

astronomers (uh-STRON-uh-murz): scientists who study the universe and all that is in it

comet (KOM-it): a small space object made up of snow, ice, and dust

constellations (KAHN-stuh-LAY-shunz): stars that, when grouped together, make a picture

galaxy (GAL-uhk-see): a large group of stars, gas, and dust held together by gravity

lunar eclipse (LOO-nur i-KLIPS): a partial or total blocking of light from the Moon caused when Earth passes between the Sun and the Moon, casting a shadow on the Moon

meteor (MEE-tee-ur): light made by a meteoroid passing through Earth's atmosphere

meteoroid (MEE-tee-ur-oid): a chunk or piece of dust from a comet or asteroid

moon phases (moon fayz-uhz): the lit part of the Moon that can be seen throughout the month

navigate (NAV-uh-gate): to lead a ship or aircraft on a planned path

solar system (SOH-lur SISS-tuhm): the Sun, planets, and everything that orbits the Sun

Index

Websites to Visit

www.nasa.gov/audience/forstudents/k-4/finditfast/K-8_Topical_Index.
   html#c

www.loc.gov/rr/scitech/mysteries/bluemoon.html

http://science.nationalgeographic.com/science/space/solar-system/

About the Author

Kimberly M. Hutmacher is the author of 24 books for children. She loves to research science topics and share what she learns. She also enjoys sharing her love of writing with audiences of all ages.

Meet The Author!
www.meetREMauthors.com